Peter Stanier was born in Cornwall and now lives in Shaftesbury, Dorset, where he is a freelance lecturer and writer on archaeology, industrial archaeology and landscapes. Peter read archaeology and geography at Southampton University, where he later received a doctorate. His main field of research is stone quarrying (he is an authority on the granite industry) and has published papers and books on the subject. He is editor of the Association for Industrial Archaeology's quarterly *Industrial Archaeology News*. His books include *Quarries and Quarrying* (1985), *Dorset's Industrial Heritage* (1989) and *Quarries of England and Wales* (1995).

Following page
A view of one of the kilns at Swanage Brickworks, Godlingston (see under Manufacturing, Bricks and Pots).

DISCOVER DORSET

THE INDUSTRIAL PAST

PETER STANIER

THE DOVECOTE PRESS

Telegrams:
"FOUNDRY,"
DORCHESTER.

LOTT & WALNE, LTD.

Telephone
National
No. 76.

MAKERS OF

AGRICULTURAL

IMPLEMENTS.

SPRING-MOUNTED

WATER CARTS

A SPECIALITY.

180 CALL. SPRING-MOUNTED WATER CART.
Write for Illustrated Price Lists.

THE FOUNDRY, DORCHESTER.

A water cart of about 1890, a typical example
of the equipment once made by
Lott & Walne in Dorchester.

First published in 1998 by The Dovecote Press Ltd
Stanbridge, Wimborne, Dorset BH21 4JD

ISBN 1 874336 55 5

Series designed by Humphrey Stone

Typeset in Sabon by The Typesetting Bureau
Wimborne, Dorset
Printed and bound by Baskerville Press, Salisbury, Wiltshire

A CIP catalogue record for this book is available
from the British Library

CONTENTS

INTRODUCTION

The great and far-reaching changes associated with the industrial age from the eighteenth to the mid-twentieth century seem to have caused little disturbance to rural Dorset. Here were no heavy industries or dark satanic mills, yet one of the delights of the county is its mix of small-scale industries, many based on natural resources. What is more, the evidence is there to be discovered.

Industries in Dorset go back a long way, and the first were those which exploited raw materials. In Purbeck, for example, Kimmeridge shale was worked from the early Bronze Age, and the Romano-British period saw shale working, potteries, salt making and quarries for Purbeck marble and Portland stone.

In medieval times there were salt-pans around Poole Harbour, at Charmouth and Lyme Regis. Quarrying had a resurgence when stone was favoured by medieval cathedral builders, while Portland stone is closely linked with Wren's late seventeenth-century St Paul's Cathedral. Glassmaking was attempted at Kimmeridge.

By the nineteenth century, small industries were flourishing throughout the county. Stone on Portland and Purbeck was quarried, especially for London, and both these districts are still active today. High quality ball clay from around Wareham came to be important. Less successful were attempts to work Kimmeridge shale for its fuel content, and ironstone at Hengistbury Head (then in Hampshire).

There was some processing of raw materials. Limeburning was widespread in limestone and chalk districts and cement was made at three sites. Bricks and tiles were made wherever there were suitable

Two examples of traditional Dorset industries in their heyday. One of Dorset's small and now extinct brickworks, the Verwood and Ferndown Brick & Tile Co. in 1890. The other photograph is of the netmaking rooms at Court Mills, Bridport, in about 1905.

clays. The so-called Verwood potteries were an example of a small rural industry, while the larger potteries became established around Poole in the later nineteenth century.

Agriculture provided the foundation for industries such as dairying or meat products, while barley found an outlet in malting and brewing. Malting has ceased but Dorset retains three working breweries. Flax from the hillsides and hemp from the valleys supplied rope and net making industries, the latter still important at Bridport. Coarse textiles, sacks and sails were also made and silk was spun in north Dorset from the mid-eighteenth century.

Manufacturing industries included paper making, for which the clear water of the chalk streams was ideal. Raw materials were flax and then old rags and ropes. There were mills at Beaminster, Wareham and Wimborne. The last to close, after 200 years, was at Witchampton on the River Allen, where a paper mill was founded in 1790.

Iron foundries in the nineteenth and early twentieth centuries supplied all manner of equipment and machinery to agricultural and other industries, sometimes far beyond the county.

Power came from water, wind and animals before the Industrial Revolution. Although harnessed mostly for corn milling, water power was also used in breweries, foundries, and flax, fulling, paper, saw and silk mills. In the nineteenth century, steam power was applied to some industries, including breweries, brickworks, corn mills, net making, waterworks and gas works.

The water, gas and electricity supply industries became increasingly important as urban development progressed throughout the nineteenth and twentieth centuries.

Two major and contrasting twentieth-century industries around Poole Harbour are the Admiralty cordite explosives factory at Holton Heath (c.1916-60) which employed up to 5,000 at its peak, and the oil exploration and extraction which began at Wytch Farm in the later part of the century.

Industry cannot function successfully without transport. There are relics of the turnpike roads, established before railways revolutionised transport in Dorset after 1847. Mineral railways were especially important on Portland and Purbeck. There were no canals,

[8]

but how different the Blackmore Vale and Stour would have been if the proposed Dorset & Somerset Canal of 1796 had succeeded. Just as important, coastal and overseas trade, ferry services and shipbuilding were served by ports and navigational aids.

Grouped under broad headings, this book outlines the more traditional industries for which something of interest remains – the 'industrial archaeology'. Each section gives a brief description, followed by a choice of sites which can be seen from a road or public footpath at the very least. Some are more accessible, but whenever in doubt, it is always courteous to ask permission to visit a site.

A reading list is given. For further investigation, a good start can be made by consulting the Kelly's Trade Directories, which show the great number of industries and crafts of the second half of the nineteenth century. Large-scale 25-inch Ordnance Survey maps of the 1900-1 revision are particularly informative as they show many industries when they were at their peak of development.

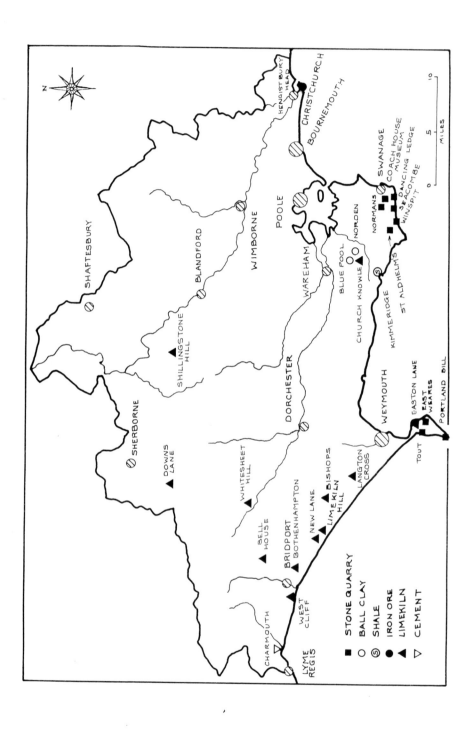

RAW MATERIALS

STONE

Stone quarrying in Dorset began with the Romans, although surface stones had been taken for building monuments ever since the
Neolithic period. Quarrying revived in medieval times and the industry saw greater developments in the eighteenth and nineteenth
centuries.

Dorset's older houses show the variety of building stones available,
taken from small local quarries now abandoned and overgrown.
Only a stone with special qualities, such as its ability to be carved,
could bear the expense of long distance carriage on poor roads. Sea
transport helped and railways later made stones more widely available outside Dorset.

Portland and Purbeck are the two most important districts for
quarrying building limestone, but stone was also quarried in the
Forest Marble and Inferior Oolites around Bridport, Beaminster and
Sherborne, and the Corallian at Marnhull. Chalk was quarried in
pits, mostly for agriculture or lime-burning. Of the sandstones, the
Upper Greensand was hard enough for building and roadmaking
around Shaftesbury.

The small island of Portland, just four miles long, is the source
of one of England's most famous stones. It had supplied a fine
white freestone for centuries, but Sir Christopher Wren boosted its
popularity when he rebuilt St Paul's Cathedral and other London
churches after the Great Fire of 1666. Since then, the industry has
hardly looked back, supplying stone by sea for many public buildings
in the capital and elsewhere. The quarries have been described by
many visitors, including John Smeaton who saw them in 1756 when
seeking stone for his Eddystone Lighthouse.

Portland's unique landscape is scarred with old and active quarries.
An overburden of Purbeck beds must be removed to reach the good

Longacre Quarry, Portland, in 1912 (British Geological Survey).

Portland roach and whitbed stones, and the waste was traditionally back-filled behind stacks of large blocks. As a result, an old quarry has masses of tipped waste and just a narrow gully representing the last working face. It is here, though, that marks of stone-cutting can be found.

The early quarries in the landslips of the east coast were served by small shipping places, but stone from the top of the island was carried down on special carts to Castletown pier. This became increasingly hazardous for man and beast, so the Merchants' Railway (see Railways) was built in 1826 when 25,000 tons of stone were being shipped every year. Convicts were brought to Portland 20 years later to quarry stone for the breakwater. Employment has always fluctuated according to demands of the construction trade. 1899 was a peak year with 1,441 quarrymen and masons recorded on the island. Competition from cheaper building materials brought decline in the twentieth century, although there was much work between the wars for memorials (including the Cenotaph in Whitehall) and war graves at home and abroad. Stone was required for rebuilding London after the last war. The decline continued but has been checked today, with a demand for quality stone for new buildings and restorations. Large stone dressing yards were set up beside the quarries. Gradually, the various stone firms amalgamated so that today there are two main groups, employing about 100. There has been much investment in mechanisation.

It is a pity that not a single old crane is left standing in any Portland quarry to symbolise the historic past. A century ago there were numerous hand-worked timber cranes all over the island. These were replaced in turn by steel cranes, first steam and then electric. Quarrying today can use powerful excavators in their place.

Purbeck is famous for Purbeck Marble, a shelly limestone which takes a polish. Worked by the Romans, it later became fashionable for decorative pillars, tomb slabs and fonts in medieval cathedrals and churches all around the country. Corfe Castle was the manufacturing centre and, although the trade has long since gone, it is still the headquarters of the Ancient Order of Purbeck Marblers and Stone Cutters. There are overgrown pits and dumps along the thin seam of Purbeck Marble all along the foot of the hill from Swanage towards Kingston. The most visible site is near Downshay Farm, on the lane between Harman's Cross and Sunnydown (SY 984796).

There have been more extensive quarries in other Purbeck beds on the high ground between Swanage and Worth Matravers, through Langton Matravers and Acton. In the 1720s, Defoe noted 'vast quarreys of stone, which is cut out flat, and us'd in London in great quantities for paving court-yards, alleys, avenues to houses, kitchins, footways on the sides of the high-streets, and the like.' There are examples of old shallow outcrop quarries in the Durlston Country Park, but the deeper beds were worked from underground 'quarrs'. At the surface, a horse-worked capstan which hauled stone up an inclined shaft was surrounded by open-fronted 'quarr houses' used for stone dressing. Only three or four men were employed. In 1907, for example, 58 quarrs had 197 workers between them. The last closed in 1963 so that all quarrying today is from the surface, using machinery.

The Purbeck-Portland cliffstone quarries were between Durlston Head and St Aldhelm's Head. Already in 1756, Smeaton observed 'they are in some measure worked underground'. Much stone was sent, for example, for Ramsgate Harbour. The quarries worked throughout the next century, but intermittently because of the difficulties of shipping. With no access inland, stone was lowered by crude cranes into small boats and ferried to larger vessels offshore. A well-known cliff quarry was Tilly Whim (SZ 031769), which was opened in the later nineteenth century as a tourist 'cave'. Now closed, it is seen from the coastal footpath.

BILL QUARRIES (SY 676684) Portland. The low tip of Portland has been quarried from the water's edge, although the stone beds are rather thin. The Pulpit Rock, left by the quarrymen in about 1875, indicates the depth of stone removed. Nearby, a small quarry can be observed safely, with a sinuous working face, piles of scappled (roughly squared) blocks and waste rock. A tramway's stone sleeper blocks lead past the lighthouse to a shipping place which has traces of cranes earlier than the present iron derrick (see Shipping). Further along the coast, some quarries have straight vertical faces where they were cut by steam channelling machines in the 1920s and 1930s. Cave Hole Quarry (SY 696691) is just inland from a timber derrick above a huge cave.

COACH HOUSE MUSEUM (SY 998789) Purbeck. The Langton Matravers Local History and Preservation Society's museum is devoted to the Purbeck stone industry and contains many items and photographs, including a reconstructed quarr. Located just behind the church, this interesting museum is a must for anyone studying the local quarries (Tel: 01929 423168). There are further exhibits in the Tithe Barn Museum, Church Hill, Swanage.

DANCING LEDGE QUARRY (SY 997769) Purbeck. Stone was lowered to a large sloping ledge and carried to a shipping place at its very edge. The carts or waggons were directed along two converging rut-ways, the grooves of which are still prominent. The quarry (partly underground) was last worked in 1914. Westwards is Hedbury Quarry (SY 992768), where square-cut holes mark the position of timber cranes for lowering stone down the cliff near an old cannon.

Capstan at the restored Norman's Quarry, Langton Matravers.

EAST WEARES (SY 703715) Portland. Acres of landslipped ground and tilting masses, with squared blocks and waste chippings to indicate quarrying sites. This was one of the first quarry areas, with stone shipped from King's, Folly and Durdle Piers. The best approach is from Church Ope Cove through Penn's Weare to Durdle Pier, down to which stone was hauled for shipment. An elderly timber crane (now for boat-handling) has iron winding gear by Galpin of Dorchester.

NORMAN'S QUARRY (SY 992789) Purbeck. Restored by the National Trust, an early twentieth-century quarr with inclined shaft, capstan between two crab-stones and two small quarr houses with stone roofs. Old quarr houses at filled-in shafts can be observed nearby.

ST ALDHELM'S QUARRY (SY 965761) Purbeck. Purbeck-Portland stone for building is still quarried by W. J. Haysom & Son who have

Underground gallery with supporting 'leg' at Winspit Quarry, Purbeck.

a stone dressing works. Here is also the last timber derrick standing in any Dorset quarry. The working quarry can be viewed from the track leading from Worth Matravers to St Aldhelm's Head. The latter has a bizarre pillar standing at the edge of an old clifftop quarry (SY 962754).

SEACOMBE QUARRY (SY 984766) Purbeck. A large quarry where Seacombe Bottom meets the coast, worked from the eighteenth century until 1923-31, when there was much investment in machinery. Underground galleries are now extremely unsafe, but outside are concrete foundations for a compressor and stone saws. Above the quarry are the foundations of steam derricks. Stone was shipped from below the west end of the quarry.

TOUT QUARRY (SY 685727) Portland. A large quarry, now a sculpture park. There are stone sleeper blocks of branches of the Merchants' Railway, and a superb stone arch, with a keystone inscribed 'J.C. Lano 1854'. Lano was the quarry manager. Two arches (one dated 1862) run beneath the Weston road into Inmosthay Quarries. Waste stone was tipped over the West Cliff, and traces of trackways and bridges can be seen crossing the clifftop footpath.

WINSPIT QUARRIES (SY 977761) Purbeck. Large cliffside quarries on both sides of the valley below Worth Matravers. There were quarries here in 1719, and they were well established when John Smeaton visited in 1756. The west quarry, which has a very wide underground gallery, was worked to about 1953. On the sea ledge below, two rut-ways lead to loading points at the water's edge. The east quarry has square-cut holes for crane positions on the cliff top above the sea and ship carvings on the walls of some of the old galleries.

BALL CLAY

Ball clay is a high grade plastic clay derived from a source much further west – perhaps Devon – and laid down in deltaic deposits of the Bagshot Beds found beneath the heaths near Wareham. Also known as 'pipe clay', it was dug in the mid-seventeenth century for making clay pipes. The following 200 years saw more clay pits opening, with exports to the Minton and Wedgwood potteries in Staffordshire. Clay was shipped from Poole to Liverpool (thence to Staffordshire) and many other ports around Britain and northern Europe. Shipments rose from 14,796 tons in 1802 to 30,485 tons in 1831 and 62,266 tons in 1851. Whereas most clay was exported in the early years, the clay began to be used in pottery and tile works around Poole after 1850.

Doulton & Co. of Lambeth worked clay pits here but the main figures in the industry were Benjamin Fayle and Pike Brothers, who built tramways (see Railways) to small quays from which their clay was barged across Poole Harbour and transhipped to larger vessels. Their headquarters were, respectively, at Norden and Furzebrook, the latter becoming the main centre when they merged in 1948 to become Pike Brothers, Fayle & Co. Ltd. Twenty years later, they were taken over by ECC Ball Clays, who continue to produce up to 200,000 tons annually.

The ball clay can be worked in open pits, after first removing an overburden of sands and poorer clays, but mining becomes necessary where the clay deposits are too deep. The older mines had vertical shafts beneath a headframe, but the few working today are inclined (drift) shafts. The clay is hard and dry underground and the miners use pneumatic spades to dig it, leaving 15 feet above to form a watertight roof. Timber props support the roof which is allowed to collapse slowly as the heading progresses. Stout wooden clay waggons of a traditional design are loaded by hand and pushed to the foot of the incline, assembled in a train and hauled to the surface where they arrive in a long building on stilts which contains a powerful winch and storage hoppers beneath. The clay is taken by lorries to Furzebrook (SY 932840) for storage, shredding and grading before it is sold. Purbeck's clay still goes to the pottery industry, for domestic and sanitary ware, electrical insulators and crucibles, while other grades are used as fillers in synthetic rubber, fertilisers and animal feeds.

BLUE POOL (SY 935833). This popular 'beauty spot' and Site of Special Scientific Interest is an unlikely industrial site, but it has been enhanced by the planting of trees after the clay-cutters abandoned their flooded pit. The deep blue or green colour of the pool is due to minute clay particles suspended in the water diffracting sunlight. A small museum shows the history of the ball clay and pottery industries *(Tel:* 01929 551408). This whole area just south of Furzebrook has been turned over for clay and there are other, less accessible, clay pits to be discovered here.

NORDEN MINE (SY 949827). A private site, worked by ECC Ball Clays, but visible from a footpath. Norden Mine is about 200 feet deep and there are two levels underground. It has two shafts (the second was sunk in 1996-7), at the surface of which there is a covered winch house, storage bins and inclined drift. There are signs of earlier clay workings here at the foot of the Purbeck Hills.

Kimmeridge is a fascinating industrial site with a long history. Shale from its cliffs was fashioned into beads, rings and armlets in the early Bronze Age and an organised 'industry' existed by the late Iron Age. The Romans used the shale for decorative furniture and wall panelling, and perhaps for fuel too.

The bituminous oil shale known as 'Kimmeridge Coal' was certainly burned locally for heating. Alum was extracted from it by boiling, for use in preparing mordants in dyeing and calico-printing, preserving skins, candle making and pharmacy. In the early seventeenth century, Sir William Clavell spent £4,000 on an alum works and pier. Others were granted the king's patent to manufacture alum, so Clavell turned to a salt works and a glass house (1617-23). The glass furnace was fueled by oil shale, but had to be dismantled after an attempt to break the monopoly which prevented sales beyond the local area.

Industry returned in the nineteenth century, with a number of commercial attempts to work the shale for its gas and oil. The Bituminous Shale Co. was here in 1848-54, with a tramway to the quay. Wanostrocht & Co. had a plant at Wareham producing gas for lamps in 1848. They won a contract ten years later to light the streets of Paris, but this was a failure! Oil and fertiliser were also produced. The Wareham Oil & Candle Co. took over the works in 1862 and other firms followed. For a while, sanitary carbon was produced to filter sewage. The last major working was in 1883-90 by the Kimmeridge Oil & Carbon Co., who built a tramway and mined the shale from the cliffs and the Manfield Shaft. The Blackstone Seam was said to yield 120 gallons of paraffin per ton. The remaining coke and carbon was used as a disinfectant and fertiliser. The high sulphur content of the shale was always a problem.

Beyond Kimmeridge, there were attempts in the early twentieth century to exploit the same oil shale beds near Weymouth, at the Manfield Shale Pit (SY 609856) near Portesham, at Corton (using German prisoners-of-war in 1917) and Westham. All proved uneconomical.

KIMMERIDGE (SY 909788). Interest centres around the shore below Clavell's Tower and the cliffs to the east. Most evidence is from nineteenth-century shale workings. The shale was mined, notably at the Kimmeridge Oil & Carbon Co.'s Manfield Shaft (SY 917783) from which a one-mile tramway ran to a wooden pier in 1883-90. There are traces of the Bituminous Shale Co.'s earlier tramway descending a cutting (SY 910787). A walk eastwards along the shore reveals old levels in the cliff face with the occasional tramway rail protruding. Another level is visible from the cliff top at Clavell's Hard (SY 920778). Cement stone was also taken·from lower levels and shipped off for making cement at Newport, Isle of Wight.

IRON ORE

Iron ore was not mined but worked opencast in a small way from local deposits in the south east after the Iron Age. Hengistbury Head (then in Hampshire) saw the only large commercial exploitation of iron ore in the mid-nineteenth century. Thankfully, iron ore at Abbotsbury was found to contain too much silica. There is an exposure in Blind Lane at SY 576856.

HENGISTBURY HEAD (SZ 176906). Ironstone occurs in the sandy beds on Hengistbury Head at the mouth of Christchurch Harbour. It must have been worked when there was a significant Iron Age trading port here. In 1848-70, the Hengistbury Head Mining Co. (managed by J.E. Holloway, a Southampton coal merchant) took ironstone in barges to Southampton to be shipped as ballast in coal ships returning to South Wales for smelting. Fallen ironstone blocks ('doggers') were first collected from the shore, resulting in the rapid erosion of the soft cliff they had protected. Large quarries were opened inland. One deep opencast, almost cutting the headland in two, has been dammed to form a pond. All along the north side, the Batters is another area of ironstone working. A few timbers protrude from the much-silted Holloway's Dock, which was the shipping place.

After burning, chalk or limestone (calcium carbonate) becomes quick-lime which reacts fiercely with water to become hydrated lime. The Romans used lime mortar for building, and there are records of its use by builders at Corfe Castle in the thirteenth and fourteenth centuries. In later years, lime was used for stucco and plaster work, white-wash, for softening water and purifying coal gas. However, most of Dorset's lime was used by farmers after the eighteenth century. The calcium in the lime neutralises acid soils, helps bacteria render fertilisers available for plant growth and improves soil texture.

Many villages or farms in all the limestone or chalk areas have a familiar 'old limekiln', often overgrown, which remains as a monument to a rural industrial phase which lasted around 200 years. Most were 'draw kilns', which could be burnt continuously for as long as required. They date from the late eighteenth or nineteenth centuries, with some larger commercial kilns built in the twentieth century. A typical kiln was built into a bank to facilitate loading from the top. Insulating walls of brick or stone enclosed a brick-lined pot which tapered towards the bottom. Broken limestone or chalk was tipped in with alternate layers of fuel, usually culm (anthracite). The charge was topped-up as burnt lime was extracted through the draw-hole at the base, reached through a draw arch in the front wall. This arch is the most striking architectural feature, and may be round (brick or stone), pointed or with a timber lintel. Commonly, a lime shed was attached to the front, to give protection from the rain.

Of over 350 known limekiln sites in Dorset, only about a quarter survive in any recognisable form. Place-names may indicate the former presence of a limekiln, such as 'Limekiln Farm' or 'Limekiln Coppice'. Interestingly, lime is still burnt in the traditional way at Shillingstone Limeworks.

BELL HOUSE (SY 499949) Loders. A fine kiln built into a hillside with a round protective wall at the top and a good surviving lime shed. Private, but visible from a lane.

The kiln and lime shed, Bell House limekiln, Loders.

BISHOP'S (SY 587858) Abbotsbury. A restored limekiln with a double timber lintel to the draw arch, adjacent to a picnic site and view point beside a lane from Abbotsbury. The kiln and its chalk pit were already disused by 1888.

BOTHENHAMPTON (SY 471915) Bothenhampton. A good example of a stone-built limekiln, cleared and restored by the local council, beside a public footpath.

CHURCH KNOWLE (SY 945822) Church Knowle. One of the best limekilns in Dorset, at the foot of Knowle Hill below a small chalk pit. It has a prominent brick draw arch with a rounded recess and a small limeburner's 'bothy' complete with its own chimney. The open pot is covered with a safety grill.

DOWNS LANE (ST 600103) Yetminster. One of several survivors around the village. A lime shed with a corrugated iron roof protects the stone draw-arch. Added interest is a wartime observation post built on top of the kiln.

EASTON LANE (SY 691727) Portland. The most visible survivor of 19 known limekilns on Portland. It is on the east side of Easton Lane, although a lime shed hides the draw-arch from the road.

LANGTON CROSS (SY 622825) Langton Herring. This fine kiln stands in a field beside a lane into the village from the B3157. Downslope (not visible from the road) the draw-arch is approached by an unusual stone-arched tunnel. The kiln is just one of several along an east-west stretch.

LIMEKILN HILL (SY 538871) Puncknowle. Preserved by the National Trust, this tall stone-built limekiln has an open pot (with safety grill) and pointed draw-arch. Shallow quarry workings behind supplied the limestone. Close to the B3157, overlooking West Bexington.

NEW LANE (SY 521880) Swyre. A small limekiln in a prominent position, an example with a pointed arch and foundations of the limeshed in front. Bumpy ground above indicates quarrying. Next to a footpath.

The remains of New Lane limekiln, Swyre.

Looking down on the hydration plant of the Shillingstone
Lime & Stone Co. Ltd.

SHILLINGSTONE HILL (ST 823098) Shillingstone. A large active chalk pit with two pairs of limekilns which have been burning since the 1930s when the hydration plant was erected by the Shillingstone Lime & Stone Co. Ltd. There are remnants of an aerial ropeway system which brought chalk down to the kilns. Today, most of the chalk is crushed for agricultural 'lime'. A public footpath passes the edge of the site.

WEST CLIFF (SY 454909) Symonsbury. This small limekiln is built into a grassed-over quarry, seen from the coastal footpath after a steep climb from West Bay.

WHITESHEET HILL (SY 586980) Toller Fratrum. A pair of commercial limekilns in the large chalk pit at Whitesheet Hill, visible from the A356 just outside Maiden Newton. Built in the 1950s with concrete blocks, they were last worked by Soil Fertility Ltd.

CEMENT

Hydraulic cement was manufactured at Lyme Regis where the Blue Lias limestone was collected from the beach and quarried from the cliffs. There was a cement factory here in 1850-1914, with a tramway out to the harbour. A smaller works at nearby Charmouth is described below. Another cement works was run by T.P. Powell at Ridge, near Wareham, in the last quarter of the nineteenth century. Chalk marl was quarried on the hill at Cocknowle (SY 933821), sent down an incline and transported to Ridge.

CHARMOUTH CEMENT MILL (SY 364930). Cement stones were gathered from the shore at Charmouth, where a small cement works and mill was erected in the 1850s. A conspicuous building remains next to the beach car park. Just behind there are granite millstones, used for grinding in the cement manufacturing process, and part of at least one limekiln.

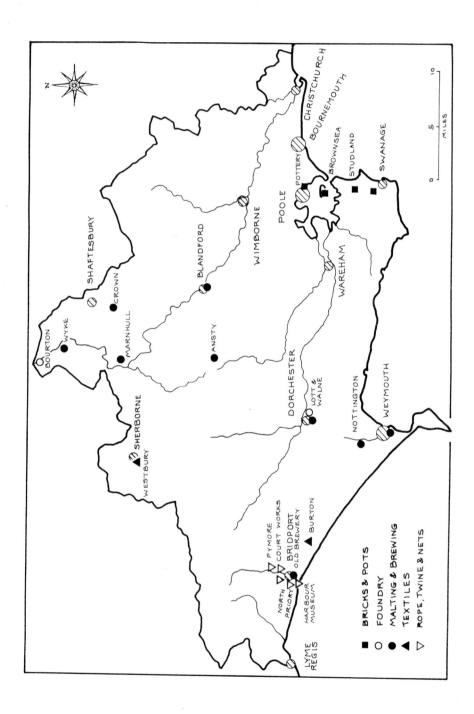

N

BOURTON

WYKE

CROWN

MARNHULL

SHAFTESBURY

BLANDFORD

ANSTY

WIMBORNE

POOLE

POTTERY

CHRISTCHURCH

BOURNEMOUTH

BROWNSEA

STUDLAND

SWANAGE

WAREHAM

DORCHESTER

LOTT & WALNE

NOTTINGTON

WEYMOUTH

SHERBORNE

WESTBURY

PYMORE

COURT WORKS

NORTH

PRIORY

BRIDPORT

OLD BREWERY

BURTON

HARBOUR MUSEUM

LYME REGIS

0   5   10

MILES

BRICKS & POTS   ■

FOUNDRY   ○

MALTING & BREWING ●

TEXTILES   ▲

ROPE, TWINE & NETS ▽

MANUFACTURING

BRICKS AND POTS

About 170 brickworks have exploited most clays in Dorset, but mainly the Oxford, Kimmeridge and younger Bagshot clays. As well as bricks of a characteristic colour and texture, a typical brickyard might also make tiles, roof finials, water pipes, drain pipes and sanitary wares. Most brickworks were in the south east, where there was the greatest demand from the builders of Poole and Bournemouth in the nineteenth and early twentieth centuries. Some became very large, even with their own tramway systems. One failure, however, was a scheme on Brownsea Island for making bricks, sewage pipes and terra cotta. Competition from other products and the introduction of plastic pipes saw many closures in the 1960s and '70s. Some clay pits had become surrounded by encroaching houses and, once abandoned, they yielded to even more development and have disappeared completely.

The expansion of Weymouth as a resort in the nineteenth century was served by local brickworks. Crook Hill at Chickerell was the last to close in 1969, but its Hoffman kiln, chimney and brick-making plant survived until 1996. Dorchester's distinctive speckled bricks came from brickworks at Broadmayne village until 1940. At Bridport, the last brickworks at Bothenhampton closed in 1959 and its clay pit became a rubbish tip. In the north, there were at least 23 brickworks in the Oxford, Kimmeridge and Gault clays across the Blackmore Vale. All were small, except for the Gillingham Pottery, Brick & Tile Co.'s works (1860s-1969) which produced harsh-coloured red bricks and owed its success to a siding from the railway at Gillingham station. The site is now an industrial estate.

Most brickyards have been demolished, leaving little physical evidence, but clues may be in place-names, such as 'Brick Kiln Plantation' at East Stoke or 'Brickyard Lane' at Bourton. The latter

still has a small kiln and a tunnel linking the clay pit and yard of the brick, pipe and tile works. Other clues come from bricks or other products impressed with their maker's name or initials. For example, old water pipes by 'R. Spencer. Sturminster Newton' are exhibited in the Museum of Water Supply at Sutton Poyntz.

Today, only two brickworks are in operation, at Godlingston near Swanage and at Corfe Mullen, where the Beacon Hill Brick Co. Ltd. makes calcium silicate (sandlime) bricks.

The Purbeck clays have been exploited commercially since at least Roman times, when there was a large trade in Black Burnished wares from the south side of Poole Harbour to military establishments as far north as Hadrian's Wall. In later times, thousands of tons were exported to Staffordshire before large-scale pottery production began around Poole. From about 1850, the Kinson Pottery was making glazed sanitary stoneware, terra-cotta goods, bricks and field drain pipes. In 1854, the Patent Architectural Pottery Co. at Hamworthy started manufacturing coloured and glazed bricks, mouldings and

[28]

The Patent Architectural Pottery Co. works at East Quay, Hamworthy, a year after it opened in 1854.

wall tiles, using a mix of local ball clay and Cornish china clay. Floor tiles were made at James Walker's East Quay Works in about 1860. Jesse Carter bought out Walker in 1873, followed by the Architectural Pottery in 1895. Floor and wall tiles and decorative pottery were produced on a large scale. Today, the Carters' Poole Pottery at the East Quay site is the only survivor.

The Verwood potteries were small rural potteries dating back to the early fourteenth century. By the seventeenth and eighteenth centuries, clay deposits were being exploited from Alderholt south-west to Horton. The potters made all types of practical earthenware, sold by hawkers ranging as far as 40 miles. The industry declined in the nineteenth century through outside competition. The Cross Roads kiln at Verwood was the last to close, in 1952. The brick-lined kilns were about 10 feet high, surrounded by a mound of earth, clay and broken pots. The Verwood & District Potteries Trust was formed in 1985 to record and preserve the remaining evidence. Collections of Verwood pottery are in the museums at Christchurch, Dorchester and Poole.

A view of the Branksea Pottery on Brownsea Island in about 1860.

BROWNSEA ISLAND (SZ 013875) Poole Harbour. In the 1850s, the island's owner Colonel Waugh hoped to produce porcelain but found the clay was only suitable for sewage pipes, sanitary wares and ornamental terra-cotta. Nevertheless, a modern pottery works was built on the south west side of the island. A horse-worked tramway brought clay from pits at Seymours on the north side and took finished products to an export pier. After financial difficulties, the works closed in 1887. There are overgrown traces of the works, while broken pipes and highly glazed bricks litter the beach and low cliffs around Shard Point. Maryland, now ruinous, was a model village of 16 workers' houses in four blocks (SZ 023883).

POOLE POTTERY (SZ 012903) Poole Quay. The Carters' well known pottery works is still in production. There is a small museum which contains displays of pottery made here and examples of painted wares from early this century, as well as a reconstructed clay mine and bottle kiln. *Tel:* 01202 669800.

STUDLAND BRICK KILN (SZ 030830) Studland. The remains of a small Scotch kiln can be seen beside Wadmore Lane, a bridleway

The remains of the Studland brick kiln.

onto Studland Heath. Little is known of the brickworks which was here from the 1890s until the early twentieth century.

SWANAGE BRICKWORKS (SY 020803) Godlingston. A rare surival of a small rural brickyard, where Wealden clays have been exploited since 1861. Ibstock Building Products Ltd. makes hand-made bricks and 'specials' of various shapes which have a higher value than common bricks. Three gas-fired down-drought kilns each have a capacity of 64,000 bricks. Not open to public, but the works and clay pit can be seen from near Ulwell.

IRON FOUNDRIES

Iron foundries or engineering works, usually of modest size, were a feature of most nineteenth-century towns, supplying agricultural machinery and a range of other cast-iron items. Some had markets for specialist products far beyond the county.

Dorset's iron foundries are listed in trade directories and, although long closed, some of their products live on. There is always the surprise of discovering a lost maker's name (and sometimes the date) cast on such diverse artefacts as agricultural implements, drain covers and gratings, lamp posts, road signs, sluices or waterwheels. From the smaller foundries, for example, there are drain covers by J. Farris & Sons of Shaftesbury and R. Old of Sturminster, a lever cheese press by Pond & Son of Blandford in the Dorset County Museum, and a Portland crane-winch and water meadow sluices at Toller Fratrum by Galpin of Dorchester. On a grander scale, Stephen Lewin's Poole foundry (1841-84) made steam launches and yachts, and small railway locomotives sold, for example, to the Goathorn Railway (Purbeck), the Guinness Brewery in Dublin and Seaham Harbour in County Durham. This, like all Poole's foundries, has been redeveloped. However, buildings survive at the two notable foundries of Lott & Walne (Dorchester) and Hindleys (Bourton), both of which had a large range of products.

The Grove Iron Works is rare survivor of a small active jobbing foundry not just in Dorset but for southern England. Here, T.J. Blackburn & Co. work in cast iron, bronze and aluminium. The older stone buildings can be seen alongside the road into Bridport at West Allington (SY 454931).

An important engineering works for manufacturing brewing equipment had its origins at Springhead, in a quiet location beneath the chalk downs near Fontmell Magna (ST 873169). Here, John Walter Flower (son of George Flower of the Fontmell Magna brewery) founded the 'Eclipse Works' in 1895, soon winning gold medals for the 'Eclipse automatic filling and corking machine' and the 'Lightning dry hopper'. Brewing machinery was designed and made for 11 years until the expanding firm moved to a larger site at Wimborne, where manufacturing continued until 1966. The Springhead Trust has established an educational centre here, but the main range alongside the millpond retains evidence of the intake for a turbine.

Foundries which supplied products from outside Dorset include E. Cockey & Sons of Frome, who made the cast-iron pillars for the Dorset County Museum's main gallery in 1883, mileposts along the A30 near Shaftesbury, and a weighbridge at Castle Farm, Buckland Newton. Dening & Co. of Chard supplied agricultural machinery and cast-iron tombs, and Joseph Armfield of Ringwood, Hampshire, made water turbines and sluices.

BOURTON FOUNDRY (ST 775310) Bourton. The foundry was established next to Daniel Maggs's corn mill and flax mill and developed by Oliver Maggs in the 1840s and '50s, for making agricultural machinery. In the 1860s, E.S. Hindley began making boilers and stationary steam engines, and by the early twentieth century, products of E.S. Hindley & Sons included steam lorries, gas and oil engines, pumps, dynamos, hoists and saw benches. There was a London office and products were exported all over the world from this small corner of north Dorset. At its height, around 200 people from the village were employed. The foundry closed in 1927, when production of the successful Hindley oil engine was transferred to Alfred Dodman's works in King's Lynn. Unemployment at Bourton was relieved when the premises became a milk products factory six years later.

The site is now a food products factory but some foundry buildings and a large mill pond survive. There were three waterwheels here. One of 1837 measuring 60 feet by 2 feet was dismantled in 1918, but its wheel pit remains as does the mark of the great wheel against a wall. Elsewhere, a cast-iron pipe by Maggs is at the Museum of Water Supply, part of an early iron waterwheel ('D. Maggs, 1819') from Nether Cerne is at the Castleton Wheel, Sherborne, while E.S. Hindley supplied waterwheels locally to mills at Cann, Melbury Abbas (1875) and Stour Provost (1889), and for pumping water at Stourhead gardens. A fine waterwheel and pump (1902) from Maiden Bradley have been re-erected at the Kew Bridge Steam Museum, London. Small Hindley steam engines are displayed at Brewers Quay, Weymouth (from the brewery) and Sherborne Museum (from the gas works).

LOTT & WALNE FOUNDRY (SY 696907) Dorchester. John Galpin founded a business here in Fordington High Street in 1840. Lott & Walne Ltd. took over in 1875, but iron-founding had ceased some time before they abandoned their premises in 1988. After remaining derelict, the nineteenth-century brick building with a crane overhanging the street has been converted to housing. Lott & Walne made their own agricultural machinery, waterwheels and sluices. Horse-drawn water carts were a speciality, sold to municipal

Lott & Walne's old foundry at Fordington, Dorchester.

authorities all over the country. In Dorchester, their name can be seen on drain covers, a stout lamp post outside the Dorchester Brewery and the superb clock tower in Borough Gardens. The Dorset County Museum has a collection of wooden patterns of 1875-1932.

MALTINGS AND BREWERIES

Dorset's beers were well known in the Middle Ages. In the fifteenth century, hops were imported into Poole from the Netherlands, while beer was exported to the Channel Islands. Dorchester had the 'best and finest beer in England' which was being sent to London by the second half of the eighteenth century. Its strength was described by Thomas Hardy in *The Trumpet Major*, when any drunk and disorderly stranger was dismissed by the magistrates 'as one overtaken in a fault that no man could guard against who entered the town unawares.'

The brewers' malt came from local barley; in 1812, Stevenson recorded malt being exported to Portsmouth and London. Barley grain was first 'steeped' in a water tank before being spread on a floor to allow germination to start. At a critical point the grain was then kilned. Before the nineteenth century, many villages had their own maltings and a small brewhouse. Marnhull, for example, had five malthouses, while Cerne Abbas was noted for its malting and brewing until the 1820s. A number of the nineteenth-century breweries built their own maltings. Weymouth has a group of large commercial floor maltings of the second half of the nineteenth century.

Beer was brewed locally at inns, and some still have their small brewhouse alongside. Private houses also had their own brewhouses, for example, Smedmore House, Kimmeridge (SY 924788).

During the nineteenth century, small breweries were established in villages and towns, but gradually these were taken over and closed by the larger breweries. There are still three brewers in Dorset: Eldridge Pope at Dorchester, Hall & Woodhouse at Blandford St Mary and Palmers at Bridport. In Dorchester, Charles Eldridge came to the Green Dragon Brewery in Acland Road in 1837. The name 'Pale Ale Brewery' above an entrance off High East Street (SY 694908), indicates a brewery acquired and rebuilt in 1854 but closed in 1883. Eldridge Pope & Co., as it became in 1871, moved to the large Dorchester Brewery in 1880. The breweries of John Devenish and John Groves at Weymouth also grew at the expense of smaller ones, but have themselves closed.

It is surprising that no brewery survived in the Poole and Bournemouth conurbation, with its large potential market. Poole Brewery in Towngate Street was owned by Frederick Styring in 1852, became Styring & Co. in 1877, but was closed by Eldridge Pope in 1899, although malting continued for a while. Bournemouth Brewery (1868-1925) in Holdenhurst Road was retained as a depot when it was bought out by Strong & Co. of Romsey. This also happened to Poole's Dolphin Brewery, Market Street, in 1926. The Christchurch Steam Brewery closed in 1934.

The maltings of Sherborne's demolished Dorsetshire Brewery in Long Street have been totally transformed into flats. At Wimborne Minster, there are traces of the Town Brewery (closed 1937 by Hall

& Woodhouse). The Julian Brewery, built in 1876 by George Habgood, was taken over in 1915 by John Groves and closed, but part can be seen behind the pub (now the Pudding and Pye). The original brewery here at the Three Lions was run by Joseph Piddle in 1848. Among the village breweries, the Sydling St Nicholas brewery (1842-1905) was bought out by John Groves. A waterwheel here was scrapped when the building was converted to a house in the 1960s.

ANSTY BREWERY (ST 764032) Lower Ansty. Hall & Woodhouse Ltd. have their origins here, where Charles Hall established a brewery in 1777. His son Robert and G.E.I. Woodhouse became partners in 1847. Brewing ended around 1900 with the opening of the new brewery at Blandford, although the maltings continued until about 1940. The brewhouse has gone, but a malthouse has been converted into the village hall near the Fox Inn.

BLANDFORD BREWERY (ST 886058) Blandford St Mary. Hall & Woodhouse Ltd.'s working brewery beside the Stour. The tall brick brewery was completed in 1900, after an earlier fire. Inside is preserved a small horizontal steam engine, built in 1899 by Gimson of Leicester to work mash tuns and hoist malt sacks. Another steam engine came from the Wyke Brewery, taken over in 1963. There is a period office building, but the large site has new facilities for brewing lager, making soft drinks and canning a wide range of products.

CROWN BREWERY (ST 867169) Fontmell Magna. An earlier brewery was rebuilt in 1876 by George Frederick Applin Flower, whose initials and date are over the door of the brewer's house. His sons continued as Flower Bros. and the brewery was taken over with 21 pubs in 1904 and closed. The brick brewery has a large lucam (hoist covering) on the wall and an iron tank on the roof made by H. Pontifex & Sons of King's Cross. It is said that the Universal Crown Cork was invented and manufactured at nearby Springhead and first used here (see Iron Foundries).

DORCHESTER BREWERY (SY 692901) Dorchester. Eldridge Pope & Co. Working. Designed by G.R. Crickmay of Weymouth and built

The Dorchester Brewery of Eldridge, Pope & Co. in 1881.

The Crown Brewery and the brewer's house, Fontmell Magna.

1880, this fine brewery was described as 'probably the finest pile of buildings devoted to industrial purposes in the south of England.' Despite a serious fire in 1922, the office block, brewhouse and maltings (disused) remain only partly altered. The bonded warehouse alongside Weymouth Avenue is exceptional, with coloured bricks used to good effect. Sidings from the London & South Western Railway gave this brewery a great advantage over all others in Dorset.

MARNHULL BREWERY (ST 780182) Walton Elm. Begun by Thomas Burt in 1821, the brewery passing through the ownership of Jennings, Jennings & Baker and Styring, White & Co., before being taken over in 1913 by Eldridge Pope. They kept the pubs and sold the brewery to Hall & Woodhouse in 1935. Although converted to housing, the tall brewery building is conspicuous when approaching Marnhull from Sturminster. Nearby, Hingarston House was the Poplar Elm Brewery of the Andrews family and John Parham before being taken over by Styring, White & Co.

NOTTINGTON MALTHOUSE (SY 661826) Nottington, near Weymouth. A three-storey malthouse built of stone, converted to residential accommodation in the 1970s, but still with its cowl, lucam and a stone inscribed 'GNS 1834'.

OLD BREWERY (SY 465921) Bridport. J.C. & R.H. Palmer have been brewing for over a century in the brewery founded in 1794. Two thatched gabled roofs are said to make this the only thatched brewery in Europe. The rear of the brewery, seen from a footpath beside the River Brit, includes a slate-roofed malt kiln of 1859, which was never used. Most striking is a large iron waterwheel (19 feet x 5 feet) made by T. Helyear of Bridport, 1879. Just inside the building is a small steam engine, by Brown & May of Devizes, Wiltshire.

WEYMOUTH BREWERY (SY 681785) Brewers Quay. Devenish's brewery closed in 1986, subsequently becoming a tourist attraction with shops and the 'Timewalk' which includes an exhibition on

Thatched roofs at the Old Brewery, Bridport.
Note the beer barrel roof finials.

brewing. The impressive brick facade of 1904 has been retained, as have two steam engines on display: by Barrett, Exall & Andrews of Reading, c.1851, and by E.S. Hindley & Sons of Bourton, c.1890. Alongside, on the corner of Hope Square and Spring Road, is the former Hope Brewery of John Groves in red brick. Cooperages, stabling and bottle stores are to the rear.

WEYMOUTH MALTHOUSES (SY 681785) Weymouth. A group of large floor maltings and their kilns in the vicinity of the Weymouth Brewery is evidence of a once-important industry here. Two malthouses were designed by the architect G.R. Crickmay: No. 2 of 1861 has storage at each end of the long malting floor, while the multistorey No. 4 (1889) has storage above as well.

The stylish Wyke Brewery, Gillingham.

WYKE BREWERY (ST 796266) Gillingham. The Matthews' architect-designed brewery was bought in 1963 by Hall & Woodhouse and closed. It was then a bottling store, became redundant and the surviving part was converted into flats. It remains 'a true Victorian brewer's castle', with twin water towers and a lucam overlooking the B3081 on the outskirts of Gillingham. There are nearby workers' cottages.

TEXTILES

Woollen textiles were never as important in Dorset as for neighbouring Wiltshire, although there was certainly a trade in the fleeces provided by the sheep of the chalk downlands (for example, Beaminster church has a carving of a wool merchant's sign). Broadcloth was made, mostly for local consumption. In the eighteenth century, a coarse white flannel known as swanskin, suitable for clothing soldiers and Newfoundland fishermen, was made in north Dorset. Over 1,200 people were said to be employed around Sturminster Newton by 1812, shortly before this trade declined, but it was a cottage industry and there were no purpose-built premises.

Locally-grown flax was perhaps more important, as it provided the source for linen textiles in the north of the county and in the west around Bridport and Beaminster. Dowlas, a coarse linen suitable for smocks, and bed ticking were made at Gillingham, Silton and Bourton; some dowlas was also made at Cerne Abbas. At the coarser end of the market, sailcloth and sacking were produced in Beaminster.

Bourton had a thriving industry in the early nineteenth century when local flax was supplemented by yarn imported from Holland. Bullpits House had been a cloth or flax mill a century before. Leats below the house were used for retting flax as well as serving the Maggs' foundry and sack manufactory (ST 775312) next to the foundry (see Iron Foundries). A second cloth mill of 1820 (ST 777309) had a waterwheel, fed from a leat and pond behind, and a steam engine. Much altered over the years, it is now a private house.

To prepare the harvested flax for spinning, bundles were first 'retted' when they were soaked in special ponds or tanks to rot away the softer material and separate the fibres. After drying, broken straw was removed by 'swingling' before the flax was combed into parallel fibres by 'heckling'. Richard Roberts erected an early flax swingling mill at Burton Bradstock in 1803.

The closest in appearance to textile mills in Dorset were the silk mills established at Sherborne and Gillingham. These were for throwing or spinning the raw silk imported from Italy and the Far East. In 1753, John Sharrer of Spitalfields converted Sherborne's Westbury Mill (a grist mill) to silk throwing and soon several hundred hands were employed in the industry. When he died in 1769, his nephew William Willmott took over, followed in the nineteenth century by his son Thomas and grandsons. The business expanded with the acquisition of Castle Mills and Middle Mill for silk throwing, and in about 1840 a new silk mill was built opposite Westbury Mill. Spinning continued at Sherborne until 1887, when the mill nearly closed. Weaving took over and, after several owners, Frederick Marsden of Coventry bought the mill in 1937 for weaving rayon. War work included weaving silk parachutes, but in 1942

Marsden introduced the weaving of fibre glass, a process continued today by CS Interglas Ltd.

The Gillingham Silk Co. was established in 1769 by Stephen Hannam, a Quaker, next to his Town Mill in the centre of Gillingham (ST 808266). He apprenticed girls from Lambeth workhouse, and they slept in a dormitory in a nearby building. Young girls were particularly suited for dealing with the extremely fine threads. The workforce rose to 150, but the business closed in 1895. After subsequent uses, the old Town Mill became empty and fire-torn before the whole site was demolished in 1988 for redevelopment. Further up Shreen Water there were other silk mills at Hincke's Mill and Lord's Mill, Mere, both in Wiltshire.

BURTON MILL (SY 490897) Grove Road, Burton Bradstock. This water-powered mill on the River Bride has been converted to housing. The wheel has gone but the sluice, by Lott & Walne of Dorchester, remains. Set in a wall is a stone inscribed: 'This flax-swingling mill, the first introduced into the West of England, was erected by Richard Roberts, 1803.' Roberts was instrumental in transforming the village's flax industry from a craft to factory basis. A terrace near the church bears the inscription 'RR 1800'.

This silk mill range at Westbury, Sherborne, dates from the 1840s.

WESTBURY SILK THROWING FACTORY (ST 635159) Sherborne. A two-storey range at the junction of Westbury and Ottery Lane (formerly Factory Lane), has the look of a small textile mill, which indeed it was, having been built in about 1840 when the Willmotts expanded their silk throwing factory from original premises over the road at Westbury Mill. Weaving later took place here before closure in the 1950s. It has been converted into small industrial units. Completing the scene is an impressive terrace of workers' houses to the north at Horsecastles, erected in the mid-nineteenth century by Robert Willmott.

ROPES, TWINE AND NETS

While flax was important for textiles, flax and hemp made Bridport the major centre for rope, twine and net making for over 800 years. A 'Bridport dagger' was once a common description for the gallows. In 1213, King John commanded 'to be made at Bridport night and day, as many ropes for ships, both large and small, as many cables as you can . . .' This established a long connection with the navy, unchallenged for four centuries until the royal dockyards erected their own ropewalks and this heavier side of the industry declined at Bridport. By the early 1800s, about 9,000 people were said to be engaged around Bridport supplying all sorts of twine, string, carpet thread, packthread, shoethread, netting, cordage and ropes, products which ranged from the finest saddlers' thread to huge cables for warships and nets for the Newfoundland fishery. Much of the net making was done by outworkers, the twine being taken to cottagers who braided the nets. By then, most of the flax and hemp was being imported into West Bay harbour from places such as Riga on the Baltic. It was cleaned by combers, before being spun into twine and twisted on rope walks.

During the nineteenth century, net-making machinery was developed and manufactured in Bridport, helping the town retain its leading position. A number of families were involved in the industry. From origins in the early seventeenth century, the two most prominent became the Gundrys (at Court, Grove and Pymore Mills) and the Hounsells (at North Mills). There were amalgamations over the years, the Hounsells becoming Bridport Industries Ltd. and then combining with Joseph Gundry & Co. in 1963 to form Bridport Gundry Ltd., still the major employer. Modern technology and artificial fibres are now used.

Bridport's rope and net making has left several industrial buildings, mostly of the late nineteenth and early twentieth centuries. They include spinning mills, covered walks for rope and twine spinning, weaving or net-making sheds, warehouses and office blocks.

COURT WORKS (SY 464931) West Street, Bridport. The headquarters of Bridport Gundry Plc. Despite a serious fire in 1949, historic survivors include the stone office block of 1844 along West Street and, at the rear, a brick warehouse with a date stone 'G. Perriman 1811'.

HARBOUR MUSEUM (SY 462895) West Bay. In a converted salt house near the harbour, the museum has displays of Bridport's rope and net making industry, including an eighteenth-century twine jack and nineteenth-century balling machine *(Tel:* 01308 420997). Research material is available in the Local History Centre at Bridport Museum, South Street *(Tel:* 01308 422116).

NORTH MILLS (SY 465935) Bridport. William Hounsell & Co.'s works, where two steam engines and a waterwheel powered machinery for making lines, twines and nets. Surviving buildings include hemp stores, covered twine walks and the old tar house. The site is now an industrial estate.

PRIORY MILLS (SY 463927) Bridport. Lines, twines and canvas were made here at Stephen Whetham & Sons' stone-built mill of the 1830s. A large round-headed window shows the position of a steam beam engine, long since scrapped. A tall stone warehouse at the corner of Rope Walks and Gundry Lane (SY 465928) belonged to the firm.

The remains of the old Pymore Mills, Bridport.

PYMORE MILLS AND VILLAGE (SY 470946). Beside the River Brit, just north of Bridport, this unique self-contained site had a flax, hemp, net and rope manufactory alongside a small village. The main flax mill, a former linseed oil, grist and balling mill, was powered by a large waterwheel but burnt down in 1959. A later mill (still used by industry), mill-pond, sluices, manager's house, office, school, and workers' houses, mostly lost to vegetation, all give a hint of Pymore's former days.

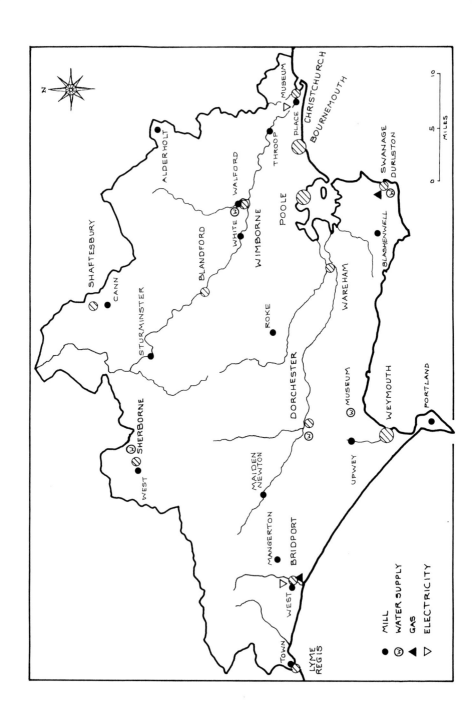

POWER AND UTILITIES

WATER AND WIND POWER

Apart from the limited application of animal power, water and wind were the prime movers for milling for centuries before the industrial period, and hundreds of known corn or grist mills have been powered by Dorset's rivers and streams. Other applications of water power include farm mills (feed milling and other agricultural purposes) and fulling, sawing, paper making, brewing, textiles and engineering works.

Most mill buildings standing today date from the eighteenth or nineteenth centuries, although some of their sites were recorded in Domesday Book – testimony to a well chosen site. A waterwheel may be undershot if there is little head of water, or breastshot or overshot when a head is provided by a mill-pond, a weir or a leat drawn from further upstream. At a corn mill, the waterwheel usually turns two or more pairs of stones, with additional drives to a sack hoist, winnower and other machinery. Loft bins feed grain by gravity to the stones on the milling floor, from where the flour is cleaned, bagged and stored on the bottom floor. There may be a covered sack hoist ('lucam') on an outside wall. Around the early twentieth century, some mills exchanged their wheels for more efficient turbines.

Some water mills have been restored – in working order, or as houses, galleries, museums or offices. Two examples of the National Trust's restoration are White Mill (see below) and Boar Mill at Corfe Castle.

There are only around 30 known windmill sites in Dorset, the first one recorded at Buckhorn Weston in 1267. Nothing survives of this or other early windmills, which were all timber post-mills. Place-names and old maps suggest sites, such as Windmill Hill (ST 717106) or Windmill Barrow (SY 937977). Windmill Knap (SZ 007801), near Swanage, is marked as 'Old Windmill' on Isaac Taylor's Map of

[47]

Dorset of 1765. A windmill at Poole is on Ogilby's Map of the Oxford to Poole Road, 1675, while the first edition one-inch Ordnance Survey Map, 1811, shows 'Cashmore Mill' on the chalk downs near Gussage St Michael. Only two structures survive in Dorset, both within a few yards of each other on Portland. Windpumps, mainly of the early twentieth century, were a specialist application for pumping water on farms and have mostly disappeared.

ALDERHOLT MILL (SU 119143) Ashford Water. The mill last worked in 1942 and was restored to produce flour in 1986 after becoming a craft shop and art gallery. The iron breastshot wheel (11 feet x 7 feet 10 inches) was made by William Munden of Ringwood. The depressing sluice is unusual.

BLASHENWELL FARM (SY 951803). A small iron farm wheel (by Munden Armfield & Co., Ringwood) is beside a building in the farmyard at Blashenwell south of Corfe Castle. A spring feeds a mill-pond behind.

CANN MILL (ST 872208) River Sturkel. N.R. Stoate & Sons Ltd. produce a wide range of flour at this working mill near Shaftesbury. It was rebuilt after a fire in 1954 but retains a wheel by Hindley of Bourton. An unusual Portuguese-style windmill was built on the roof in 1971. The next site downstream, French Mill, is now a house. Upstream, Melbury Abbas Mill has a Hindley wheel dated 1875.

MAIDEN NEWTON MILL (SY 596977) River Frome. A large iron wheel (15 feet x 12 feet) by Winter & Hossey of Dorchester on the west end of the building replaced two internal wheels. The mill was later a carpet factory and engineering works.

MANGERTON MILL (SY 490957) Mangerton River. Two wheels (12 feet x 4 feet) drove a grist mill on the north side and a flax mill on the other. The latter became a saw mill, its wheel replaced by a turbine, but is now disused. The corn mill, which last worked in 1966, has been restored and is open to the public with a small museum and a tea room.

Wind and water power at Cann Mill, near Shaftesbury.

PLACE MILL (SZ 160924) River Avon. This small mill contains some early stonework, having belonged to Christchurch Priory until 1539. It worked until the early twentieth century, and has since been restored and opened as a craft centre. A leat comes from the Avon, although the tailrace falls into the Stour.

PORTLAND WINDMILL TOWERS (SY 690713 & SY 691712). Portland has no streams, but the windswept plateau top was ideal for windmills. There are two well-preserved stone towers at Cottonfields and Top Growlands near Easton. Possibly dating from the seventeenth century, they are marked on a map of 1710 and worked until the 1890s.

The mill at Roke Farm on the Bere Stream, Bere Regis.

ROKE FARM (SY 835960) Bere Stream. This wheel (22 feet x 4 feet) cannot be missed, being next to a lane just north west of Bere Regis. It worked machinery in a farm building of 1880, but is unusual in being so close to the source of a stream. It was restored in 1985.

STURMINSTER NEWTON MILL (ST 782135) River Stour. A stone and brick seventeenth and eighteenth-century mill at a picturesque location, beside a weir above Sturminster Bridge. Two undershot wheels (the latest by Munden of Ringwood in 1849) were replaced in 1904 by one of Joseph Armfield's 'British Empire' turbines. Restored milling machinery is demonstrated at work. Upstream are Cut Mill (ST 776165), at a large weir and reached from Hinton St Mary, and King's Mill (ST 766172), a solid three-storey building next to King's Mill Bridge near Marnhull. Downstream is the small Fiddleford Mill (ST 801136) which has a stone inscription dated 1566 built into a wall.

THROOP MILL (SZ 113958) River Stour. A substantial brick mill, rebuilt in 1912 and powered by an Armfield turbine which draws

A view of the sluices on the River Stour upstream of Throop Mill.

water from a broad weir and sluices upstream. A mill on this site was owned by Quarr Abbey (Isle of Wight) in the eleventh and twelfth centuries, and some flour was manufactured into ships' biscuits nearby in the nineteenth century.

TOWN MILL (SY 342922) River Lim. Mill Lane, Lyme Regis. A Trust has been returning the mill to working order with the installation of a waterwheel (12 feet x 4 feet) and renovation of buildings for a gallery, craft workshops and restaurant. The old mill had two waterwheels, replaced by a single one before a turbine was used for generating electricity in the early twentieth century.

UPWEY MILL (SY 663851) River Wey. Seen alongside Church Street, Upwey, this fine stone-built mill of 1802 has four floors and an impressive waterwheel (22 feet x 9 feet) which is fed by two streams at different levels.

WALFORD MILL (SU 009007) River Allen. Stone Lane, Wimborne. A mostly nineteenth-century brick building, on the site of an earlier mill. There is some evidence for two internal undershot wheels, and a tall chimney stack was for a steam engine supplying additional power. The Walford Mill Craft Centre has been here since 1986. Elsewhere in Wimborne, an old millstone at the end of Mill Lane is a clue to the site of the Town Mill (SU 011001).

WEST MILL (SY 463931) River Brit. West Street, Bridport. A well-built brick mill of 1880, with a prominent lucam and cast-iron window frames, on the site of a corn and balling mill (the north wing remains). Much of the machinery, including the original turbine by Hick Hargreaves of Bolton, was retained inside the building when it was converted to an architect's office.

WEST MILL (ST 632154) River Yeo. Located at the end of West Mill Lane, Sherborne, and near the sewage works, this small stone-built mill is sadly derelict but has an external iron wheel of 1877.

The external iron wheel at West Mill, Sherborne.

The wooden pitwheel, wallower and spur wheel before conservation at
White Mill, Sturminster Marshall on the River Stour.

WHITE MILL (ST 958006) Sturminster Marshall, River Stour. A
large brick mill of 1776 which worked until 1944. The mill has been
restored to a display condition by the National Trust. There were
two mills under one roof and although their waterwheels have gone,
the late eighteenth-century wooden machinery inside is of special
interest. The miller's house is to the north and the fine medieval
White Mill Bridge to the south.

WATER SUPPLY

Although hand pumps or small cast-iron fountains continued to be
sufficient for village water supplies, the demand for good quality
piped water which accompanied the growth of larger towns saw the
birth of the water supply industry during the nineteenth century. All
Dorset's water is extracted from rivers, springs or boreholes.

The first important works and pumping station was the Weymouth Waterworks Co.'s Sutton Poyntz site, authorised by an Act of 1855. A second steam pumping station at Gould's Hill, Upwey, has now gone, but the nearby Friar Wadden Pumping Station still operates. The Bournemouth Gas & Water Co. of 1863 first took water from a stream at Bourne Valley, then outside the town. This was abandoned in 1889, when there was a water extraction site and pumping station at Longham; Walford Bridge (Wimborne) followed. A large treatment and reservoir site at Alderney was expanded in 1893-1902 and several times since. They are still operated by the Bournemouth & District Water Co. Elsewhere, at Swanage, works promoted by George Burt include a fine water tower of 1886 at Durlston and a covered reservoir at Ulwell, commemorated in 1892 by a tall granite obelisk on Ballard Down above (SZ 022813).

CASTLETON PUMPING STATION (ST 646169) Sherborne. A stone building near the railway line contains a waterwheel (26 feet x 3 feet 9 inches) made in 1898 by Edward White of Redditch to replace a wheel driving three vertical ram pumps supplied in 1869 by Stothert & Pitt of Bath. These worked until about 1960 and were scrapped. The large wheel has been restored by the Castleton Waterwheel Restoration Society and is open to the public on occasions.

DORCHESTER WATER TOWER (SY 684906). This dominant iron reservoir tank on a brick-arched tower was built in 1881 for the Dorchester Corporation. It stands on high ground at the west end of town, off Bridport Road and Wessex Road.

DURLSTON WATER TOWER (SZ 032782) Swanage. In the same architectural style as George Burt's 'Durlston Castle', this substantial stone structure, 45 feet high, complete with turret, can be recognised as a water tower by the writing 'Swanage Water Works' on the side. Opened 1886, water was pumped up to a lead water tank, from which it was distributed to Swanage by gravity. The tower is now part of a house and can be seen from Purbeck Terrace Road, off Bon Accord Road. The Swanage Water Works building is in Sentry Road (SZ 033786).

Dorchester's superb water tower of 1881

The stone water tower at Durlston, Swanage.

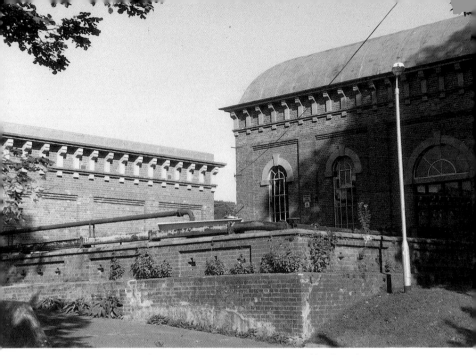

Wimborne Pumping Station, near Walford Bridge.

MUSEUM OF WATER SUPPLY (SY 706839) Sutton Poyntz. The Weymouth Water Co.'s works and pumping station opened in 1856, with later buildings added for new pumping engines. Redundant buildings have been given over by Wessex Water to a museum containing pumps, engines and other artefacts of the water industry. These include an original turbine made by David Cook & Co. of Glasgow. The manager's house is a former mill-house. A path leads to the springhead under the chalk escarpment, where the reservoir overflow and filter used part of a funnel from Brunel's *Great Eastern*, bought when the ship put into Portland Roads after an explosion on her maiden voyage in 1859. This fascinating piece of history is still there. *Tel:* 0117 929 0611.

WIMBORNE PUMPING STATION (SU 007009) Walford Bridge, Wimborne. A 'cathedral' of the water industry, with handsome brickwork and half-domed roofs. It was erected in 1896-1904 by the Bournemouth Gas & Water Co. to obtain pure water from deep underground for Bournemouth. Simpson compound tandem steam pumping engines were replaced in 1959 by electric pumps. Treatment plant was installed to soften the water and remove mineral deposits.

GAS AND ELECTRICITY

Coal or town gas was first used for street lighting, but domestic lights, cookers and heaters became more common in the 1850s. Dorset's first gas works was opened in 1832 by the Bridport Gas Co. (established 1831). Eventually, there were also gas works at Beaminster, Bournemouth, Dorchester, Gillingham, Lyme Regis, Shaftesbury, Sherborne, Stalbridge, Sturminster Newton and Weymouth.

The Bournemouth Gas & Water Co.'s first gas works (1863) at Bourne Valley was replaced in 1924-6 by a modern works with 136 vertical retorts, built on reclaimed mudflats near Poole Quay, where it received coal direct from ships. After nationalisation in 1949, a mains grid enabled Poole to supply outlying towns, resulting in the gradual closure of the smaller gas works. With the coming of North Sea gas, all town gas-producing works were demolished and redeveloped. However, a few traces of the industry remain, such as offices, houses and smaller ancillary buildings. The only surviving gas holder is a large one at Weymouth. Sherborne Museum has a small No.5 Alcazar steam engine (E.S. Hindley & Son, Bourton, 1925) which drove tar and liquid pumps for the Sherborne Gas & Coke Co., some of whose buildings survive near the railway station. Some gas lights still illuminate the lane near Throop Mill (see Water and Wind Power).

A rival to gas, electricity came much later to Dorset, first from local generators in towns in the early twentieth century. Christchurch's old power station is now the Southern Electric Museum, with a very comprehensive collection. Elsewhere, the Blandford Forum Museum has a fully restored dynamo which supplied the first domestic electricity in the town.

Poole Power Station, with its twin 325-foot chimneys, was Dorset's largest industrial building and could be seen from miles aound Poole Harbour before demolition in 1993-94. Planned before nationalisation by the Bournemouth & Poole Electricity Supply Co., it was built in 1949-52 on the Hamworthy side of Holes Bay, first generated in December 1951 and eventually had six generator sets with a capacity of 340,000 kw – small compared with modern stations. It began as a coal-fired station, but was soon converted to oil, both fuels arriving in coasters which had to pass through Poole Bridge.

BRIDPORT GAS WORKS (SY 465923) South Street. Dorset's first gas works, where town gas was made from coal from 1832 until 1958. The first cast-iron horizontal retorts were made by the Neath Abbey Iron Co. The site has been cleared, but Bridport Gas Co. buildings in local stone survive on each side of the old entrance: the manager's house (datestone 'BGC 1872') and the showroom (1899).

BRIDPORT POWER STATION (SY 463933) St Swithins Road. The Municipal Electric Power Station at Allington was built by George Abbot & Son in 1929. No longer used for its original purpose, the distinctive brick building with clerestory roof is now occupied by Nicholson Engineering Ltd.'s church bell works.

Bridport Power Station of 1929.

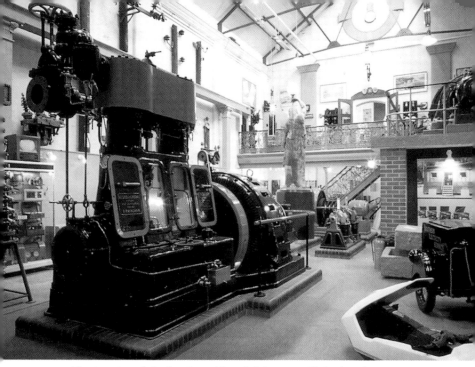

The interior of the Southern Electric Museum, Christchurch.

SOUTHERN ELECTRIC MUSEUM (SZ 156931) Bargates, Christchurch. This is the only museum devoted to the electricity industry, with an impressive display of over 500 exhibits in the engine and and boiler houses of the former power station (1903-26). They explain over a century of development of the electricity supply industry. There are replicas of early laboratory equipment, generators, switchgear, transformers, appliances, lighting and wiring systems. Large exhibits include a Bellis & Morcom/GEC steam generating set and a generator and Armfield turbine from Ringwood's hydro-electric station. *Tel:* 01202 480467.

SWANAGE GAS WORKS (SZ 020792) Victoria Avenue. The main stone retort house is a workshop for Greystone Garage. Alongside the road, a small building has a stone engraved: 'SWANAGE GAS WORKS BUILT 1867, rebuilt 1882. Established 16 and 17 Victoria ch 16'. There was a rail siding from the Swanage Railway in 1885.

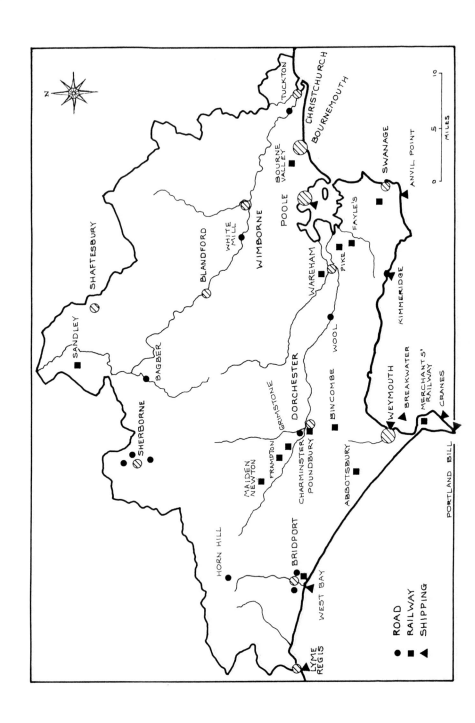

TRANSPORT

ROADS

Commerce and industry cannot function without the means of transporting raw materials and finished products overland, by packhorse, cart, waggon or lorry. Hand-in-hand with the Industrial Revolution, turnpike trusts set out to improve an existing network of poor roads. Acts of Parliament directed the trustees, usually landowners and merchants, to invest money to improve, maintain or make new routes, for which they could raise tolls. The trusts were renewed by Acts every 21 years which allowed extensions and branches. Twenty trusts were created in Dorset between 1752 and 1857. Some crossed into neighbouring counties, and vice versa.

The Shaftesbury & Sherborne Trust (Act 1752-3), along the mail route from Salisbury to Exeter, now the A30, was followed by the Harnham, Blandford & Dorchester Trust (1753-4), now the A354, and the Poole Trust (1755-6). The extensive Blandford & Poole Trust (1764-5) was divided into two in 1824-5, the northern division becoming the Vale of Blackmoor Trust with its several branches. In the west, the Bridport First and Second Districts (1764-5) covered the area around Bridport. Central Dorset had the Weymouth, Melcombe Regis & Dorchester Trust (1760-1) and the large and important Maiden Newton Trust (1777-8). The Puddletown & Wimborne Trust (Act 1841) came just before the first railway to Dorchester opened in 1847, and its backers (notably the Drax family of Charborough Park) lost heavily. Nevertheless, this late trust filled in gaps between Bere Regis and Wimborne, now followed by the busy A31. Few trusts were a financial success, but their achievement was to establish the present road network. The last trusts were abandoned in 1882, six years before the new Dorset County Council took over the roads.

Features to look out for are embankments, cuttings, bridges, tunnels, tollhouses, milestones, mileposts, direction posts and miscellaneous street furniture. Bridges are of all periods. Good medieval examples on the Stour and its tributaries not described below include Cornford (ST 692120), Crawford (ST 919020), Julian (SZ 003998), Sturminster (ST 784135), and the packhorse bridge at Fifehead Neville (ST 772111). In contrast, there are the twentieth-century lifting harbour bridges at Poole and Weymouth, or the wartime Callendar-Hamilton bridge erected by Canadian Army engineers in 1942 at Twofords Bridge, Lydlinch (ST 751138), and still in use. Cast-iron notices placed on bridges include the famous threatening 1828 ones: 'DORSET. ANY PERSON WILFULLY INJURING ANY PART OF THIS COUNTY BRIDGE WILL BE GUILTY OF FELONY AND UPON CONVICTION LIABLE TO BE TRANSPORTED FOR LIFE BY THE COURT 7 & 8 GEO4 C30 S13 T. FOOKS'. Later examples warn drivers of traction engines and 'other ponderous carriages' that bridges are 'insufficient to carry weights beyond the ordinary traffic of the district.'

Dorset can be proud of its two rare tunnels, built in 1832 by the Bridport First and Second Trusts, at Thistle Hill (SY 348948) near Charminster, now by-passed by the A35, and at Horn Hill near Beaminster.

Tollhouses, which stood opposite a tollgate, were single or two-storeyed with a bay front. Being small and on the roadside, relatively few have survived as homes without alteration or demolition. A large board was displayed listing tolls for every conceivable vehicle or animal. Four exist from the Vale of Blackmoor Vale Trust: on the tollhouse at South Cheriton (ST 693248) in Somerset, in Gillingham Museum (two) and the Salisbury & South Wiltshire Museum.

Trusts recorded the distances on milestones and mileposts of their own styles. Milestones were carved with the distance to towns (examples at Blandford and Wareham include Hyde Park Corner) and sometimes the date. Others were fixed with a cast-iron plate. Fully cast-iron mileposts are usually later in date.

'Street furniture' includes finger guide or direction posts (Dorset's finial-topped ones are 1940s-60s), post boxes, lamp posts, fountains, drinking troughs and telephone kiosks. Dorset has the oldest pillar box in use in England, at Barnes Cross near Holwell (ST 693117).

Four of Dorset's many milestones and mileposts.

2
DORCHESTER
BY THE NEW ROAD
**MAIDEN
NEWTON**
6

**POOLE
TRUST**

5 5
CRAN- **WIM-**
·BORNE **·BORNE**

9
To
POOLE
110
To
Hyde Park
Corner

Blandford
I
Dorchester
15

Left A gas lamp at Throop Road, Holdenhurst, Bournemouth.
Right The 1853 pillar box at Barnes Cross, Holwell.

Made in 1853, it has a vertical letter slot with weather flap. A later hexagonal Penfold pillar box is at the corner of South Street and South Walks in Dorchester. The 1921-designed 'K1' telephone kiosk at Tyneham (SY 882803) is worth noting for its rarity.

BAGBER BRIDGE (ST 764156) River Lydden. Designed by W. Dawes and supplied by the famous Coalbrookdale Co. in about 1850, this bridge is on a minor road (once important) between Sturminster and Stalbridge. It has cast-iron beams with wrought-iron tie-rods beneath, between stone abutments.

BRIDPORT TOLLHOUSES. There is a large brick tollhouse of the Bridport First Trust on West Road, West Allington (SY 457930). A brick house at the Skilling Hill Road junction opposite Palmer's Brewery is also believed to be a tollhouse (SY 466922).

CHARMINSTER TOLLHOUSE (SY 675921) A37 near Dorchester. A 'classic' six-sided tollhouse of two storeys, on the Maiden Newton Trust's 'New Road' which by-passed Charminster, as recorded on a milestone at SY 671929.

HORN HILL TUNNEL (ST 467032) A3066, near Beaminster. The 345-foot long tunnel avoided the steep climb over Horn Hill, thus improving the turnpike between south Somerset and west Dorset. It was built in 1831-2 to the design of Michael Lane, a pupil of the Brunels at the Thames Tunnel. An inscription over the portals praises Giles Russell of Beaminster for seeing the project through.

SHERBORNE TOLLHOUSES. There are small tollhouses on the A30 at Oborne (ST 651177), the B3145 at Whitepost (ST 640193) and an impressive one at Westhill on the A352/A3030 junction at the top of Sherborne Hill (ST 643145). There are associated mileposts on all these roads.

The tollhouse at Westhill, at the top of Sherborne Hill.

TUCKTON BRIDGE (SZ 149923) River Stour. An early reinforced concrete bridge of Mouchel-Hennebique design, 347 feet long with 11 spans. It was built in 1905 to replace a timber toll bridge of 1883 and carried twin tram tracks from Southbourne to Christchurch. It was a toll bridge until 1943.

WHITE MILL BRIDGE (ST 958005) River Stour. The finest medieval bridge on this river, said to date from 1175. Built of heathstone, limestone and greensand, it has eight round arches, with cutwaters and refuges for pedestrians above each pier. On a lane from Sturminster Marshall.

WOOL OLD BRIDGE (SY 845872) River Frome. A fifteenth-century stone bridge, repaired in 1607 and the eighteenth century, close to Woolbridge Manor, depicted in Thomas Hardy's *Tess of the d'Urbervilles*. Just downstream is the concrete bridge abutment of the old military railway to Bovington Camp.

RAILWAYS

Dorset's four main Victorian railways brought increased commercial and passenger traffic to the towns along their east-west and north-south routes. In 1847, the Southampton & Dorchester Railway (London & South Western Railway) entered the county via Ringwood, Wimborne and Wareham. It was planned to continue to Falmouth, so the first Dorchester South Station was aligned to the west. Ten years later, the broad-gauge Wiltshire, Somerset & Weymouth Railway (Great Western Railway) reached Weymouth via Yeovil and Dorchester. The Dorchester to Weymouth section was shared with the LSWR as mixed-gauge until 1874.

The Salisbury & Yeovil Railway (the LSWR's Waterloo to Exeter line) opened in 1859-60 with stations at Gillingham, Sherborne and Yeovil Junction. Fifteen years later, the Somerset & Dorset Joint Railway was formed from the Dorset Central and Somerset Central Railways. The former had been built from Wimborne northwards in 1860-62. Freight continued to Blandford for three years after the line closed in 1966. Affection is still felt for the old S&DR whose course can be traced across the Blackmore Vale and through the Stour Valley. All closed lines and branches have left much of interest to explore, including old stations, bridges and earthworks.

Railway developments around Poole began with a Hamworthy branch until a direct line to the town was opened from Broadstone in 1872. The Salisbury & Dorset Junction Railway came to West Moors through Alderholt and Verwood in 1866. The exclusive resort of Bournemouth was content with two stations on lines approaching from the opposite Poole and Christchurch directions, until these were linked in 1888 to become the through line.

There were five branch lines to the coast. The Bridport Railway (1857-1975) from Maiden Newton was continued to West Bay in 1884 (closed to passengers in 1930). The Weymouth & Portland Railway (1865-1965) crossed to Chesil, but only in 1900 was the Easton & Church Hope Railway extended through landslips and a cutting to the top of Portland. The Swanage Railway (1885-1972) from Wareham carried holiday passengers as well as local clay and stone. Upon closure, the rails were lifted back to the Furzebrook clay and oil terminals, and restoration has been under way ever since. The Abbotsbury Branch (1885-1952) from Broadwey was less successful. Most of the Lyme Regis Railway (1903-1965) was in Devon, being a branch from the LSWR at Axminster.

There were also military railways, with short branches to the signals camp at Blandford (1918-21), the tank training camp at Bovington (1919-28) and into the Portland naval dockyard.

Mineral railways in Dorset date from 1806, and in many ways these are the most interesting. Three Purbeck lines took ball clay to quays on Poole Harbour: the Fayle or Middlebere Tramway, Pike Tramway and Goathorn Railway. A tramway on Brownsea Island connected a pier, clay pits and brick and pipe works in the 1850s. Tramways at Kimmeridge served the shale workings and a pier, and there was a short inclined tramway to chalk and marl pits at Cocknowle (SY 933821). The rails of the Swanage Pier Railway of 1859 for carrying stone can be seen along the sea front at Swanage (SZ 033787).

Portland had the greatest concentration of tramways, with around 13 miles in 1901. The Merchants' Railway carried thousands of tons

Bincombe Tunnel.

of stone to the shipping quay at Castletown. The inclined Breakwater Railway supplied stone for the breakwater construction. At the Bill, a short line led to a shipping place.

ABBOTSBURY BRANCH. There are no major earthworks on this 5-mile branch of 1885-1952, but well-built stone station buildings survive at Abbotsbury, Portesham and Broadwey. Watery Lane passes beneath a bridge arch near the last. A branch incline curved up to Portesham quarries (SY 610859).

BINCOMBE TUNNEL (SY 673855). One of the best tunnels in the south, where there was no other option but to tunnel beneath the high Ridgeway Hill. It is 814 yards long and a stone portal and a deep cutting are seen from the A354 as it descends to Upwey.

BOURNE VALLEY VIADUCTS (SZ 062922). Two large viaducts, in brick with stone details, converge at Branksome. The east viaduct was closed in 1967 but the other still carries the main line from Bournemouth to Poole. A huge embankment was made with material excavated by steam navvy from the long cutting to the east, when the final link was made in 1888.

FAYLE'S TRAMWAY. A 3½-mile horse-worked plateway of 3 feet 9 inches gauge, built by Benjamin Fayle in 1806-7 to carry ball clay from Norden to Middlebere Quay. There are stone sleeper blocks at a cutting and embankment on Hartland Moor (SY 961851), now part of a footpath named the Hartland Way. The portal of one of two tunnels beneath the A351 near Norden at SY 948832 has a datestone 'BF 1807'. The tramway ceased in 1905 when the steam Goathorn Railway (1868-1936) was extended from Newton to take clay to the deepwater Goathorn Pier.

FRAMPTON TUNNEL (SY 631951). A 'cut-and-cover' tunnel across a long cutting to maintain the landowner's property. Now single, it had twin broad gauge tracks of the WSWR, and can be seen from Church Lane at Frampton.

Two views of Fayle's Tramway. *Left* The course of Fayle's Tramway, Hartland Moor. *Right* The now flooded and overgrown remains of the tramway tunnel of 1807.

Looking up the incline of the Merchants' Railway from Castletown, Portland, in about 1910.

GRIMSTONE VIADUCT (SY 640945). A solid stone bridge for the WSWR has a large central arch flanked by two lesser ones. At the turning to Sydling St Nicholas from the A37.

MAIDEN NEWTON STATION (SY 599980). A country station with flint and Ham stone buildings which give the air of having been important, for it was the junction for the Bridport branch.

MERCHANTS' RAILWAY. The Merchants' Railway (1826-1939), 4 foot 6 inch gauge and horse-worked, was built to carry the increasing tonnages of stone from the Portland quarries. A crane at Priory Corner loaded stone brought by road and there were quarry branches. Stone-laden trucks were delivered to Castletown Pier down the Incline, from the top of which (SY 689738) two lines with sleeper blocks curve around the Verne to a complex of four bridges (with datestones 1875-82) and an incline at SY 692733.

PIKE TRAMWAY. Pike Brothers built a 2 foot 8 inch gauge line in 1838-40 to take clay from Furzebrook to Ridge Wharf on the River Frome. Horse-drawn at first, steam locomotives were introduced in 1866, with Latin numbers from *Primus* onwards. Branches can be traced across country to the south west from their old Furzebrook headquarters. The straight line to Ridge Wharf crosses the Arne lane at SY 937863. After closure, the *Secundus* locomotive of 1874 found its way into the Birmingham Museum of Science and Industry in the city where it was built.

POUNDBURY TUNNEL (SY 682912). A shallow tunnel glances under the corner of Poundbury hillfort as the WSWR approaches Dorchester. A cutting would have sufficed, but public outcry won the day and this was the solution to save the ancient site. The Roman aqueduct is also of interest here.

SANDLEY TUNNEL (ST 775247). West of Gillingham, LSWR engineers encountered difficult geological conditions when driving this tunnel in 1859. The east portal is seen from a lane crossing the line.

SWANAGE RAILWAY. A steam railway, with locomotives and rolling stock in use or under restoration. The original station terminus buildings with booking halls, etc, are at Swanage (SZ 029789) and a

Swanage Railway engine shed and turntable.

West Bay Station before final closure in 1962.

small engine shed with a turntable is visible from an overbridge (Northbrook Road). Corfe Castle has a station and stone viaduct with four arches across the Studland road (SY 960825). Nearby can be seen a sloping iron bridge of the old clay tramway and a two-arched stone bridge under the Arne lane where the two lines ran parallel (there were exchange sidings here).

WAREHAM STATION (SY 920881). A Victorian station in brick, with stone dressings including the LSWR's coat of arms and 1886 date. The platform canopies have decorated cast-iron posts. Built for the opening of the Swanage branch, it replaced the first station where an engine shed still survives.

WEST BAY STATION (SY 465904). A stone station with tall chimneys was built for the Bridport branch extension of 1884 to receive the projected holiday trade. The branch closed for passengers in 1930 and for goods in 1962. Having become dilapidated, this delightful building and its platform have been restored for offices and an information centre for West Dorset District Council's proposed West Bay harbour improvements.

The sea has provided a means of transport since prehistoric times, not least the Iron Age when there was a trading port at Hengistbury Head. Most visible evidence, however, dates from the industrial age. Poole and Weymouth are the largest ports with a true maritime flavour, with warehouses, cranes and repair yards. Other ports were Lyme Regis, West Bay and Swanage, with many lesser places around the coast involved in local trade and fishing. The naval dockyard at Portland has left a legacy after over a century's use.

Raw materials were shipped from some improbable places, requiring skilful navigation and calm weather. Stone was loaded from the exposed Portland and Purbeck cliffs, and shale from jetties at Kimmeridge. Ball clay and iron ore were shipped from small timber quays and a dock, now lost beneath silt in the shallow waters of Poole and Christchurch Harbours.

Lighthouses, navigational aids, coastguard lookouts and houses are further aspects of the archaeology of the shipping industry. Few places can boast three lighthouses at one spot, like Portland Bill where there was also a lightship marking the Shambles offshore. Houses for lighthouse keepers and coastguards (as at Brownsea Island and St Aldhelm's Head) were built in a particular style.

ANVIL POINT LIGHTHOUSE (SZ 029769). Situated 100 feet up the cliffs, this lighthouse only required a short tower when it was built in 1881. The adjoining keepers' accommodation is surrounded by a wall in Trinity House fashion.

KIMMERIDGE (SY 909788). A ruined stone pier or breakwater was built in 1860 by Wanostrocht & Co. for shipping shale. Traces of the Kimmeridge Oil & Carbon Co.'s wooden pier of 1883 project from the sea wall.

LYME REGIS (SY 339915). The artificial harbour at Lyme is protected by the curving Portland stone breakwater known as the Cobb. First recorded in 1372, when it was destroyed in a storm, it

An aerial view of the Cobb, Lyme Regis.

has seen major repairs following storms in 1792, 1817 and 1824. Victoria Pier (1829) extends from the Cobb. Used mainly for coastal trade, blue lias limestone and cement were exported in the nineteenth and early twentieth centuries. The harbour's seaward position is due to erosion and recession of the cliffs behind.

POOLE QUAY (SZ 009903). Of interest at the heart of old Poole, are the Customs House (1813), Harbour Office (1822) and the Town Cellars, a fifteenth-century woolhouse now part of the Waterfront Museum. Later warehouses have been converted for tourism. The lifting Poole Bridge (1927) allows road traffic to cross to Lower Hamworthy, which is busy with repair yards, coastal shipping and a ferry port.

PORTLAND BILL LIGHTHOUSES (SY 677684). Portland Bill has three lighthouses. The coal-fired Higher and Lower Lights of 1716 worked together. Rebuilt in 1789, the Lower Light was the first to

Poole Quay from Hamworthy Docks.

use a true lens, while the Higher Light was the first in the country to have an Argand oil lamp. The towers seen today (SY 681690 and SY 677693) are rebuildings of 1869. A day-mark erected by Trinity House in 1844 on the low tip of the Bill is now dominated by the 136-foot high lighthouse of 1906 which replaced both older lighthouses. When open, visitors can see the fog signal air compressors as well as the light after a long climb to the top.

PORTLAND BREAKWATER (SY 706750). This great breakwater encloses a huge harbour. Designed by James Rendel and finished by Sir John Coode, the first breakwater was built in 1849-72, when nearly 6 million tons of Portland stone were sent down the inclined Breakwater Railway from the convict quarries. The breakwater is cut by the South Ship Channel, the ends of which are in Cornish granite. The threat of torpedo attacks led to the final two arms being added in 1895-1903, with an iron lighthouse on the end of the north eastern breakwater. The Royal Naval dockyard under the Verne

The lighthouse on Portland Breakwater.

Old stone-shipping cranes on Portland.

heights at Castletown closed in 1996. Castletown Pier (SY 687744), built of large stone blocks, served the stone trade. Across the harbour at Wyke Regis, the last part of the Whitehead Torpedo Works was demolished in 1997.

PORTLAND CRANES (SY 680685 to SY 705717). There were stone-shipping places all along the east coast of Portland, either natural ledges above deep water or crude quays as at Durdle Pier. That trade has gone but the foundations of earlier cranes lie alongside derricks now used for launching fishing boats. Makers' names cast on the winches include Butters Bros. of Glasgow on an iron crane at the Bill and Galpin of Dorchester on an older timber crane at Durdle Pier. Other cranes are at Cave Hole and Sandholes.

SWANAGE (SZ 035787). Swanage was a stone port long before a tourist resort. Stone kerbs and setts were stored along the seafront awaiting shipment to London. The Old Pier of the Swanage Pier & Tramway Co. was opened in 1859, but was in a poor state when the railway came in 1885 and has since almost vanished. The New Pier (1893-5), with a double deck, was for passenger paddle steamers and restoration work has been carried out by the Swanage Pier Trust.

WEST BAY (SY 462904). The mouth of the Brit – Bridport Harbour – often became choked with sand and gravel, so a harbour with sluices and piers of the 1740s was developed in 1823-5. Hemp, timber and coal were imported and beach gravel exported, but ships no longer pass through the twin entrance piers. The few warehouses have found other uses, and the Harbour Museum (with a display on the harbour) is in a converted salt house. Wooden ships were built on the west side in 1779-1885. The name West Bay dates from the coming of the railway and attempts to create a resort.

WEYMOUTH (SY 680787). The old warehouses along the harbour have been converted for the tourist trade but the place retains its feel of a bustling harbour. The fish ice house of 1855 is of interest, and along the quay is the old tramway which brought trains to the cross-channel ferry terminal.

FURTHER READING

Addison, J. & Wailes, R., 'Dorset Watermills', *Trans. Newcomen Society*, vol XXXV, 1962-3, 193-216

Algar, D, Light, A. & Copland-Griffiths, P., *The Verwood and District Potteries: A Dorset Industry*, Ringwood, 1979; 2nd ed, 1987

Anon, *Poole Pottery: The First* 100 Years of the Story of Poole Pottery, 1873-1973, Poole Pottery, 1973

Benfield, E., *Purbeck Shop: a Stoneworker's Story of Stone*, new edition, Ensign Publications, 1990

Bone, M., 'Bridport Textile Industry 1814-1945', *Somerset & Dorset Notes & Queries*, vol XXXI, Sept 1981, 141-154

'The Bridport Flax and Hemp Industry', *Bristol Industrial Archaeology Society Journal, vol* 18, 1986, 19-31

'Dorset Windmills', *Somerset & Dorset Notes & Queries*, vol XXXIII, March 1995, 360-363

Chubb, L., et al, *Dorset Toll-House Survey*, Dorset County Council, 1977

Copland-Griffiths, P. & Butterworth, C., 'Excavations of the 17th century kiln at Horton, Dorset', *Procs. Dorset Natural History & Archaeological Society*, vol 112, 1990, 23-32

Crossley, D., 'Sir William Clavell's Glasshouse at Kimmeridge, Dorset: The Excavations of 1980-81', *Archaeological Journal*, vol 144, 1987, 340-382

Davies, W.K.J., *Pike Bros, Fayle & Co Ltd, Furzebrook*, Narrow-gauge Railway Society, 1957

Dewar, H.S.L., 'The Windmills, Watermills and Horsemills of Dorset', *Procs. Dorset Natural History & Archaeological Society*, vol 82, 1960, 109-132

Eedle, M. de G., *Horn Hill Tunnel*, author, 1994

Good, R., *The Old Roads of Dorset*, Commin, 1966

Hawkins, J., *The Poole Potteries*, Barrie & Jenkins, 1980

James, J., *Dorset Turnpike Roads*, Dorset Archaeological Committee, 1995

Lucking, J.H., *Dorset's Railways*, Dovecote Press, 1982

Maggs, C.G., *Branch Lines of Dorset*, Sutton Publishing, 1996

Morris, S., *Portland: an illustrated history*, Dovecote Press, 1985

Otter, R.A. (ed.), *Civil Engineering Heritage: Southern England*, Thomas Telford Ltd., 1994

Phillips, J., 'Quarr Houses on the Isle of Purbeck, Dorset', in P. Newman (ed.) *The Archaeology of Mining and Metallurgy in South-West Britain*, Peak District Mines Historical Society & Historical Metallurgy Society, 1996, 155-162

Popplewell, L., *Ironstone Canyon: The Hengistbury Head Mining Company*, Melledgen Press, 1986

Ross, M.S., 'Brickmaking at Gillingham and Motcombe, Dorset', *Procs. Dorset Natural History & Archaeological Society, vol* 113, 1991, 17-22

Sanctuary, A., *Rope, Twine and Net Making*, Shire Publications, 1980

Saville, R.J., *Industrial Archaeology and Transport of Purbeck*, Globe Education, 1976

    Langton's Stone Quarries, Langton Matravers Local History & Preservation Society, 1976

Seekings, J., *Thomas Hardy's Brewer: the story of Eldridge Pope & Co.*, Dovecote Press, 1988

Stanier, P., *Dorset's Industrial Heritage*, Twelveheads Press, 1989

    Quarries of England & Wales, Twelveheads Press, 1995

    'The Quarried Face: evidence from Dorset's cliffstone quarries', in P. Newman (ed.) *The Archaeology of Mining and Metallurgy in South-West Britain*, Peak District Mines Historical Society & Historical Metallurgy Society, 1996, 1-9

    'Dorset Limekilns: a first survey', *Procs. Dorset Natural History & Archaeological Society* , vol 115, 1993, 33-49

    'More Dorset Limekilns', *Procs. Dorset Natural History & Archaeological Society*, vol 117, 1995, 91-94

Stevenson, W., *A General View of the Agriculture of Dorsetshire*, 1812

Trim, P., *The Quarrying of Portland Stone*, Island of Portland Heritage Trust, 1991

Wallis, A.J., *Dorset Bridges, A History and Guide*, Abbey Press, 1974

Wear, R. & Lees, E., *Stephen Lewin and the Poole Foundry*, Industrial Railway Society, 1978

Young, D., 'Brickmaking in Dorset', *Procs. Dorset Natural History & Archaeological Society*, vol 93, 1971, 213-242

    'The Architectural Pottery', *Procs. Dorset Natural History & Archaeological Society*, vol 92, 1970, 212-213

Young, J., *Old Dorset Brewers*, Better Pubs Ltd., 1986

The

DISCOVER DORSET

Series of Books

A series of paperback books providing informative illustrated
introductions to Dorset's history, culture and way of life.
The following titles have so far been published.

All the books about Dorset published by The Dovecote Press
are available in bookshops throughout the county,
or in case of difficulty direct from the publishers.
The Dovecote Press Ltd, Stanbridge,
Wimborne, Dorset BH21 4JD
Tel: 01258 840549.